UPDATED

ISBN 0-7935-1063-5

This publication is not for sale in the E.C. and/or Australia or New Zealand.

7777 W. Bluemound Rd. P.O. Box 13819 Milwaukee, WI 53213

BLUE EYES

Words and Music by ELTON JOHN
and GARY OSBORNE

Em7 -5
A+
A
A+
A
Dm
and I say
I will see
(1) Blue eyes hold-ing back the tears
(2,3) Blue eyes laugh-ing in the sun,
Bb/D
F
F/A
Fm/Ab
hold-ing back the pain
laugh-ing in the rain
ba-by's got blue
ba-by's got blue
Gm
Eb11
1 Bb/C
C
eyes, and she's a-lone
eyes, and am I home
a-gain.
F
Eb
Ab
Gb
Db/F
Ab/Eb
Eb
Fine
2 Bb/C
C
D.S. al Fine
And am I home a-gain.
Fine

BENNIE AND THE JETS

Words and Music by ELTON JOHN
and BERNIE TAUPIN

C
G
(3rd time vocal) Say
Can - dy and Ron - nie have you seen them yet but
(no solo 3rd time)
Am
C
they're so spaced out
Ben - nie and the Jets
G
Am
But they're weird and they're won - der - ful oh Ben - nie She's real - ly keen
She's got e -
C
D
Em
Em7
lec - tric boots a mo - hair suit you know I read it in a mag - a - zine oh

C
Bb/C
D
Gmaj7
G6
Gmaj7
To Coda
Ben - nie and the Jets
Fmaj7
G7
Fmaj7
G7
1
Fmaj7
G7
Fmaj7
Am/G
2
Fmaj7
G7
Fmaj7
Am/G
D.S. (Piano solo) al Coda
CODA
Gmaj7
Ben - nie Ben - nie
Fmaj7
G7
Fmaj7
G7
Fmaj7
G7
Fmaj7
Am/G
Repeat and Fade
Ben - nie Ben - nie Ben - nie Ben - nie and the Jets

BORDER SONG

Words and Music by ELTON JOHN
and BERNIE TAUPIN

F
F♯dim
C/G
F6/G
To Coda
Ho - ly Mo - ses, I have been re - moved.
Ho - ly Mo - ses, I have been re - moved.
He's my broth - er, let us live in peace.
C
F
1
C
2
C
F
C
F
I'm go - in' back to the bor - der where my af - fairs, where
C/G
F/G
C
F
my af - fairs ain't a - bused, I can't take an - y more bad wa - ter been

D/F#
F6/G
poi - soned from my head down to my shoes.
Oh!
C
F
C
F/C
G/B
D.S. al Coda
CODA
C
oh
F
F#dim
C/G
F6/G
C
he's my broth- er
let us live in peace
oh
G7sus
Dm7
C
F
C
F
C
let us,
let us live in peace.

CANDLE IN THE WIND

Music by ELTON JOHN
Words by BERNIE TAUPIN

E
A
wood-work and they whis-pered in - to your brain.
died, oh, the press still hound-ed you.
E/G#
They set you on the tread - mill and they made you change your name.
All the pa - pers had to say was that Mar - i - lyn was found in
A
D/A
A
B
B7
the nude.
It seems to me you lived your life like a
E
A
E
can - dle in the wind, nev-er know-ing who to cling to when the

B
Bsus
2 fr
B
A
rain set in.
I would have liked to have known
C♯m
4 fr
you, but I was just a kid.
Your can - dle burned out
B
Bsus
2 fr
B
A
long be - fore
your leg - end ev - er did.
A/G♯
F♯m7
E
3

B
A
A/G♯
F♯m7
E
Esus
E
1
B
B7
2
B
B7/A
E
Good-bye Nor - ma Jean,
A
though I nev - er knew you at all you had the grace to
E/G♯
A
D/A
hold your - self while those a - round you crawled.

A
E
Good-bye Nor-ma Jean, from a young man in the
A
E/G♯
twen-ty sec-ond row who sees you as some-thing more than sex-ual, more than
A
Asus
A
just our Mar-i-lyn Mon-roe. It
B
B7
E
E7
seems to me you lived your life like a can-dle in the wind,

A
E
never knowing who to cling to when the rain
B
Bsus
2fr
B
A
set in.
And I would have liked to have known
C#m
4fr
you, but I was just a kid.
Your candle burned out
B
Bsus
2fr
B
A
long before
your legend ever did.

A/G# F#7 E E7/G#
I
A C#m
would have liked to have known you, whoa, but I was just a kid.
B
Your can - dle burned out long be - fore
Bsus B A A/G# F#m7 E
your leg - end ev - er did.
rit.

EMPTY GARDEN
(Hey Hey Johnny)

Words and Music by ELTON JOHN
and BERNIE TAUPIN

Bb
Cm
good crop.
Now it all looks strange.
It's fun-ny how one
Ab
Bb
in - sect
can dam-age
so much grain.
Eb
Ab
And what's it for, this
thru their tears
8va
loco
R.H.
L.H.
lit-tle Emp-ty Gar-den by the
some say he farmed his best in
Eb
brown - stone door?
young - er years,
And in the cracks a-long the
but he'd have said the root grows

Bb
Cm
side - walk,
noth - ing grows no more.
Who
strong - er.
If on - ly he could hear.
Who
Ab
Eb
lived here?
He must have been a gar - den - er who cared a lot, who
lived there?
He must have been a gar - den - er who cared a lot, who
Bb
weed - ed out the tears and grew a good crop.
And we are so a - mazed,
weed - ed out the tears and grew a good crop.
Now we pray for rain.
Cm
Ab
we're crip - pled and we're dazed.
A gar - den - er like that
And with ev - 'ry drop that pours,
we

Bb
Eb
one, no one can re - place.
hear, we hear your name
And I've been
Ab
Eb
knock - ing, but no one an - swers. And I've been
f
Ab
Cm
knock - ing most all the day. Oh, and I've been
Fm
Cm
To Coda
call - ing, oh, hey, hey John - ny, can't you come

Ab
Bb
Eb
out
to play?
8va
pp R.H.
D.S. al Coda
And
loco
CODA
Can't you come out,
Ab
Bb
Eb
Fm
can't you come out
to play?
John - ny,
Ab
Bb
Eb
Fm
Repeat and Fade
can't you come out to play
in your Emp - ty Gar - den?
John - ny,

CROCODILE ROCK

C
D
and skim-min' stones Had an old gold Chev - y and a
nights cry - in' by the rec - cord ma - chine dream - in' of my Chev - y and my
G
place of my own But the big - gest kick I ev - er got was do-in' a
old blue jeans But they'll nev - er kill the thrills we've got burn - ing
Bm
C
thing called the croc - a - dile rock while the oth - er kids were rock - in' round the
up to the croc - a - dile rock learn - ing fast till the weeks went past
D
clock We were hop - pin' and bop - pin' to the croc - a - dile rock, Well
We real - ly thought the croc - o - dile rock would last, Well

Em
A7
Croc-o-dile rock-in' is some-thing shock-in' when your feet just can't keep still,
D7
G
I nev-er knew me a bet-ter time and I guess I nev-er will
Oh
E
A7
Lawd-y ma-ma those Fri-day nights when Su-sie wore her dres-ses tight and
D7
C
the croc-o-dile rock-in' was out of sight.

G
Em
C
D
1
2
3
But the years
I re - mem -
G
Em
C
D
Repeat and Fade

DANIEL

Words and Music by ELTON JOHN
and BERNIE TAUPIN
Moderately bright
mf
C
Dm
1.4. Dan - iel is trav - 'ling to - night on a plane
2. They say Spain is pret - ty 'though I've nev - er been
3. Instrumental ad lib. at 1st D.S. (small notes)
G
I can see the red tail - lights
Well Dan - iel says it's the best place he's

E7
Am
F
head - ing for Spa in Oh and I can see Dan -
ev - er seen Oh and he should know
G
Am
- iel way - ing good bye God it looks
he's been there e - nough Lord I
F
G7
F/G
To Coda
like Dan - iel Must be the clouds in my eyes
miss Dan - iel Oh I miss him so much
1
C

2
C
F
Oh
Dan-iel my broth - er you are
C
F
old-er than me do you still feel the pain
Of the scars
C
Am
that won't heal your eyes have died
But you see more than I
F
Fm
C
A7
Dan - iel you're a star
In the face of the sky

Dm7
G7
D.S. twice
1st D.S. Instrumental
ad lib. (small notes)
2nd D.S. 1st lyric again
al Coda
CODA
C
Oh God it
F
looks like Dan - iel
G7
F/G
Must be the clouds in my eyes.
C
F
G
C
F
C

DON'T GO BREAKING MY HEART

Words and Music by CARTE BLANCHE
and ANN ORSON

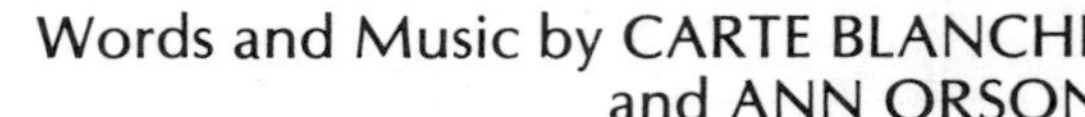

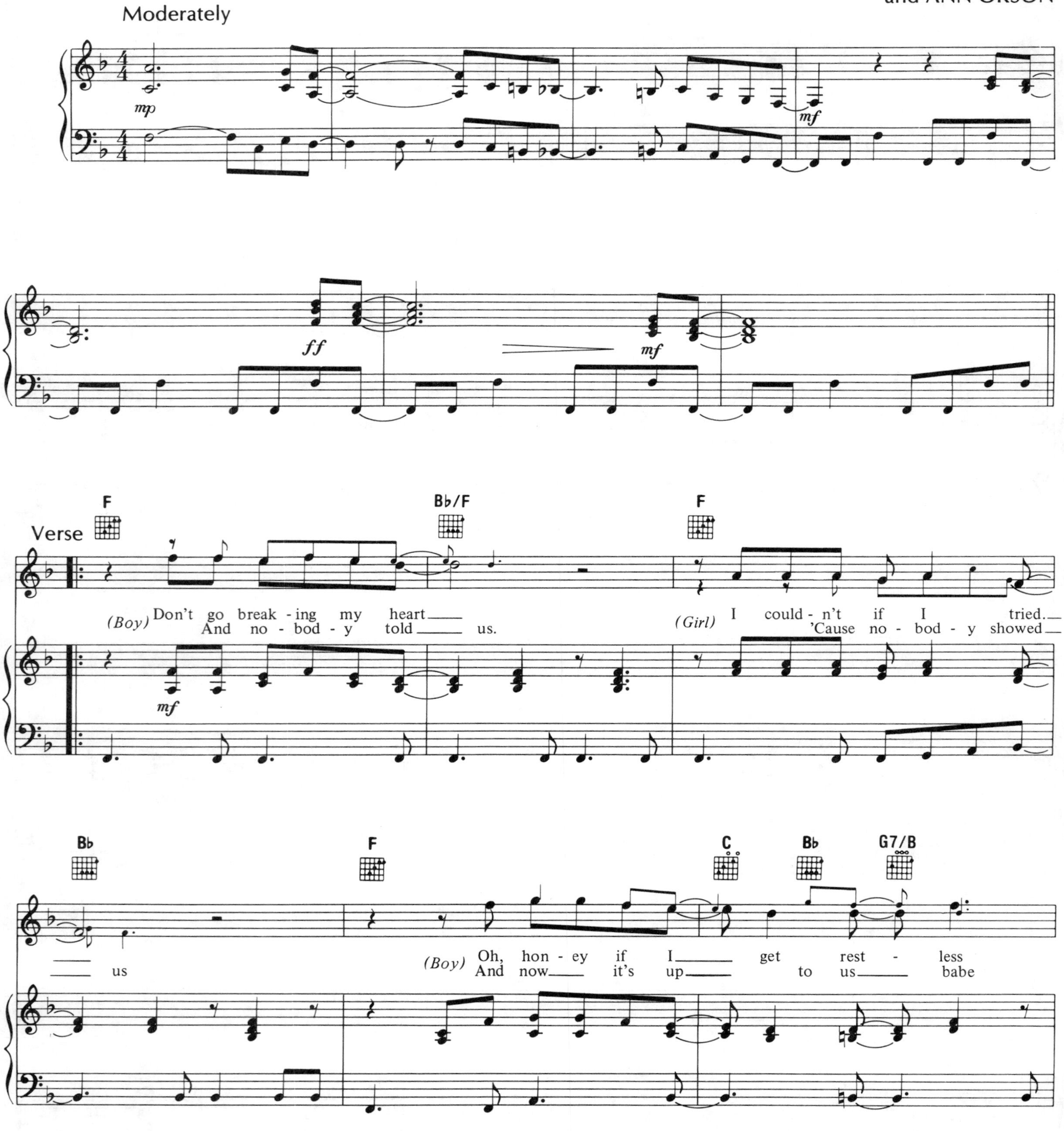

Moderately
mp
mf
ff
mf
Verse
F
Bb/F
F
(Boy) Don't go break - ing my heart
And no - bod - y told us.
(Girl) I could - n't if I tried.
'Cause no - bod - y showed us
mf
Bb
F
C
Bb
G7/B
(Boy) Oh, hon - ey if I get rest - less
And now it's up to us babe

F/C
B♭
F
B♭
F
B♭
C7
(Girl) Ba - by you're not that kind
Oh, I think we can make it.
F
B♭/F
F
(Boy) Don't go break - ing my heart
So don't mis - un - der - stand me
(Instrumental 3rd time)
(Girl) You take the weight off me
You put the light in my life
B♭
F
B♭
G7
(Boy) O hon - ey when you knock at my door.
Oh you put the spark to the flame.
F/C
B♭
F
B♭
(Girl) Ooo I gave you my key
I've got your heart in my sights

Am
Cm7
Chorus
(Together)
Oo oo
No-bod-y knows it
(Boy) But
f
Bb
F
C
G
Am
when I was down
(Girl) I was your clown
(Together) Oo oo
No-bod-y knows
Cm7
Bb
F
C
G
it, no-bod-y know - ows it.
(Boy) Right from the start
(Girl) I gave you my heart
Ab
C7/E
Bb/F
F
Bb
F
Bb
C7
Oh oh I gave you my heart

F
Dm
B♭
C7
To Coda
F
C7
(Boy) So, don't go break-ing my heart
(Girl) I won't go break-ing your heart
Dm
B♭
C7
F
B♭
(Together) Don't go break-ing my heart
F
1 B♭
2 B♭
D.S. al Coda
mp
CODA
F
(Together) Don't go break-ing my
Dm
1 B♭
C7
2,3,4 B♭
C
Repeat ad lib and Fade
Don't go break-ing my
Don't go break-ing my heart
(Girl) I won't go break-ing your heart

DON'T LET THE SUN GO DOWN ON ME

Words and Music by ELTON JOHN
and BERNIE TAUPIN

F/C
C
F/C
C
C7/E
F
me.
Fro-zen here
On the lad-der of my
G
C/G
G7
C/G
G7
life.
Too late
to save my-self from
C
F/C
C
C/E
F
B♭/F
F
fall - ing.
I took a chance
and changed your way of life
G
C/G
G
G7
But you mis-read
my mean-ing when I
F/C
C
C/E
F
met you.
Closed the door
and left me blind

C/G G F/G C C/B♭
-ed by the light Don't let the sun go down on me
Am7 D7/F♯ C/G
al-though I search my-self it's al-ways some-one else I see I'd just al-low a frag-ment of your
F/G G7 C C/B♭ F/A
life to wan-der free But los-ing ev-'ry thing is like the
Dm C/E C/G F/G To Coda C C/B♭ F/A C/G
sun go-ing down on me.
F G G7 C
I can't find oh the right ro-man-tic line.

C/E
F
But see me once
and see the way I feel
G7
C/G
G7
C/G
G7
Don't dis-card me
Just be-cause you think
C
C/E
F
I mean you harm
3
But these cuts I have
oh they need
C/G
G
G7
D.S. al Coda
love
to help them
heal
CODA
C
me.
C/B♭
F/A
A♭
B♭
C
ritard

GOODBYE YELLOW BRICK ROAD

Bb
Eb
C7
F
I'm not a pre - sent for your friends to o - pen this boy's too young to be
mon - grels who ain't got a pen - ny Sing - ing for tit - bits like
Db
Eb7
Ab
sing - ing the blues
you On the ground
Ah
Db
Bbm
C7
F
Ah
So good - bye yel - low brick
A7
Bb
F
D7
road Where the dogs of so - ci - et - y howl
You can't plant me in your pent -

Gm
C7
F
Dm
house I'm go - ing back to my plough
Back to the howl - ing old owl
A
Bb
Db
Eb
in the woods Hunt - ing the hom - y back toad
Oh I've fin -
F
Am
Dm
Bb
C7
Db
- 'ly de - cid - ed my fu - ture lies
be - yond the yel - low brick road
Eb
Ab
Db
Bbm
Ah
Ah
C7
1
F
2
F
Ah
Ah

I GUESS THAT'S WHY THEY CALL IT THE BLUES

Words and Music by
ELTON JOHN, BERNIE TAUPIN
and DAVEY JOHNSTONE

B7
Em
G7/D
C
bust out the de - mons in - side, and it won't be long be-fore you and me
cry in the night if it helps, but more than ev - er I simp - ly love
G
Am
F
G
run, to the place in our hearts where we hide.
you, more than I love life it - self.
Am7
G7/B
C
G/B
F
And I guess that's why they call it the blues. Time on my
C
G
F
C
G
hands could be time spent with you, laugh - ing like chil - dren, liv - ing like

Am
C/E
F
D/F♯
lov - ers, roll - ing like thun-der un - der the cov - ers, and I
F
/G
1-2
C
Em
F
guess that's why they call it the blues.
3
C
G
Am
Em
F
/G
blues, laugh-ing like chil - dren, liv - ing like lov - ers, and I guess that's why they call it the
C
G
Am
Em
F
/G
C
blues. And I guess that's why they call it the blues.

HONKY CAT

Words and Music by ELTON JOHN
and BERNIE TAUPIN

Brightly, with spirit

D7
Look-in' for an an - swer, try - in' to find a sign,
G
un - til I saw your cit - y lights, hon - ey I was blind. They said,
B7
get back, hon - ky cat, bet - ter get back to the woods well I
E7
quit those days and my red - neck ways and a,
D7
hmm, hmm hmm, hmm, hmm,
oo, oo, oo oo, oo,
oh, the change is gon - na do me good.

G
(Xyl.)
You bet - ter
B7
get back, hon - ky cat liv - in' in the cit - y ain't where it's at, it's like
E7
try'n' to find gold in a sil - ver mine, it's like
D7
To Coda
try'n' to drink whis - key oh, from a bot - tle of wine.
G
(Xyl.)
Well I

D7
read some books and I read some mag - a - zines a - bout those
G
high class la - dies down in New Or - leans and all the
D7
folks back home, well, they said I was a fool. They said,
G
oh, be - lieve in the Lord is the gold - en rule. They said
B7
get back hon - ky cat, Bet - ter get back to the woods, well, I

E7
quit those days and my red - neck ways and
D7
oo, oo, oo, oo, oo, oh, the change is gon - na do me good.
G
(Xyl.)
1
They said,
2
They said,
D7
stay at home, boy, you got - ta tend the farm,
G
liv - in' in the cit - y boy, is, is gon - na break your heart.

D7
But how can you stay, when your heart says
G
no, ah, ah, how can you stop when your feet say go.
D.S. al Coda
You bet-ter
CODA
(Xyl.)
D7
Get back, hon - ky cat, get back, hon - ky cat,
G
get back, ooh.
Repeat and Fade

I'M STILL STANDING

Words and Music by ELTON JOHN and BERNIE TAUPIN

2,3
Am7
Am
Em7
Don't you know, I'm still stand - in' bet - ter than I ev - er did
Dm9
Fmaj7
look - in' like a true sur - vi - vor, feel - in' like a lit - tle kid.
G
Am7
Am
Em7
And I'm still stand - in' af - ter all this time
Dm9
Dm7
E7
pick - in' up the piec - es of my life with - out you on my mind.

Verse 3
Once I never could hope to win
You starting down the road
Leaving me again, The threats
you made were meant to cut me down
And if our love was just a circus
You'd be a clown by now.

LUCY IN THE SKY WITH DIAMONDS

Words and Music by JOHN LENNON
and PAUL McCARTNEY

F
A/E
A/G
F#m
A
To Coda
slow - ly a girl with kal - eid - o - scope eyes.
flow - ers that grow so in - cred - ib - ly high.
turn - stile the girl with kal - eid - o - scope eyes.
Dm7
Cm7
Bb
C
Cel - lo - phane flow - ers of yel - low and
News - pa - per tax - is ap - pear on the
loco.
F6
Bb
green tow - er - ing o - ver your head
shore wait - ing to take you a - way
C9
G
D7
Em7
Look for the girl with the sun in her eyes and she's
Climb in the back with your head in the clouds and you're

Dm
G
C
D
Slow 4
gone.
gone.
Lu - cy in the sky with dia - monds,
ff
Lu - cy in the sky with dia - monds,
Lu - cy in the sky with
dia - monds
Ah
D.S. al Coda
CODA
Lu - cy in the sky with dia - monds,
Lu - cy in the sky with dia - monds,
Lu - cy in the sky with dia - monds,
Ah
A
Repeat and Fade

LEVON

Moderately slow, with a beat

Words and Music by ELTON JOHN
and BERNIE TAUPIN

F
Bb/F
F
Bb
Le-von, Le-von likes his mon-ey
Je-sus he wants to go to Ve-nus.
He makes a lot they say
Leave Le-von far be-hind
F
C/E
Spends his days
Take a bal-loon and go
Dm
Am
Bb
count-ing in a ga-rage by the mo-tor way.
sail-ing, while Le-von Le-von slow-ly dies.
Gm7
Am
Dm
He was born a pau-per to a pawn on a

Bb
F/A
Gm7
F
Christ - mas day when the New York Times said God is dead and war's be - gun.
Bb
F/A
Gm7
Guitar Tacet
Al-vin Tos-tig has a son to - day. And he shall be Le -
Bb
F/A
- von. And he shall be a good man. And he shall be Le -
Bb
F/A
- von in tra - di - tion with the fam - 'ly plan and he shall be Le -

Bb
F/A
Bb
To Coda
von.
And he shall be a good man.
He shall be Le-
C7sus
C
F
Bb/F
F
von.
Bb/F
C7sus
C7
D.S. al Coda
von.
And he shall be Le-
CODA
C7sus
C7
von.
F
Bb/F
F
Bb
Repeat and Fade

NIKITA

Words by BERNIE TAUPIN
Music by ELTON JOHN

D
G
C/G
G7
G7/B
and nev - er find a warm - er soul to know.
Nik - it - a do you count the stars at night?
Oh, I saw you by the wall,
And if there comes a time
C
Dm/C
F/C
C
G
Am/G
Ten of your tin sold - iers in a row;
guns and gates no long - er hold you in,
G
D
G/D
D7
with eyes that looked like ice on fire,
and if you're free to make a choice,
the hu - man heart a cap - tive in
just look to - wards the west and find
G
C/G
G7
G7/B
C
Dm/G
the snow.
a friend.
Oh Nik - it - a, you will nev - er know

C
G
an - y - thing a - bout my home. I'll nev - er know how good it feels to
D
G/D
D7
G
C/G
hold you. Nik - it - a, I need you so.
G7
G7/B
C
Dm/G
C
Oh Nik - it - a, is the oth - er side of an - y giv - en
G
C/G
G
D
Em
D7/F#
line in time count - ing ten tin sold - iers in a row? Oh no, Nik - it - a you'll

G
Bm
Bm7
C
To Coda
C#dim
Dsus
D
nev - er__ know.__
G
Bm
Bm7
C
F/C
C
C
G(add 9)/B
G/B
F/A
Bb
Eb
3-

Ab6/Eb
G7/D
Cm
Ab
D7sus
D7
D.S. al Coda
Oh Nik - it - a, you will nev-
CODA
Am7
D7
G
Count - ing ten tin sold - iers in a row.
Bm
Bm7
C
Am7
D7
Repeat and Fade
Nik - it - a.
Count - ing ten tin sold - iers in a

SAD SONGS
(SAY SO MUCH)

Words and Music by ELTON JOHN
and BERNIE TAUPIN

G
C/G G
C
rough spots__ is the hard - est part when mem - o - ries re - main.
word makes sense,__ then it's ea - si - er to have those songs a - round.
And it's times____ like these__ when we all______ need__ to hear__ the ra -
The kick in - side_____ is in____ the___ line______ that fi - nal - ly gets__
F
Bb/F F
G
di - o,____ 'cause from the lips_____ of____ some__ old sing-
___ to___ you.__ And it feels so good to hurt so bad__
C
- er we can share the troub - les we al - read y know.
and suf - fer just e - nough to sing____ the blues,_____

(So) Turn 'em on, turn 'em on, turn on those
F
Bb
F
G
sad songs. When all hope is gone why don't you
C
F
C
tune in and turn them on? They reach in - to your
F
Bb
F
room, oh, just feel their gen - tle touch.

G
To Coda
When all hope is gone
a sad song says so much.
C
C
Sad songs, they
F
Bb/F F
Dm
G
say,
sad songs, they say,
C
F
Bb/F F
Dm
sad songs, they say,
sad songs, they

G
C/G
G9
C/G
D.S. al Coda
say so much. So turn 'em on
CODA
C
F C
When all hope is gone you know a sad song says so much.
G
G9
C
F C
When ev - 'ry lit - tle bit of hope is gone you know a
G
sad song says so much.
G9
C
F C
Dm/C
C

PHILADELPHIA FREEDOM

Words and Music by ELTON JOHN
and BERNIE TAUPIN

G7
Fm6/Ab
Gm7
F
The less I say the more my work gets done.
Chorus
Bb
F
'Cause I live and breathe this Phil-a-del-phi-a free-dom
f
Bb
F
From the day that I was born I waived the flag
Eb
D7
Gm7
Phil-a-del-phia free-dom took me knee-high to a man
Eb7
D7
Db
Bb
Yeah! Gave me peace of mind my dad-dy nev-er had.

F
Bb
Oh, Phil - a - del-phi - a free - dom shine on me I love
Am7
Gm7
Am7
G7/B
C7
it. Shine the light through the eyes of the one left be - hind.
Em7/A
A7
Gm7
Am7
Shine the light, shine the light. Shine the light Won't you
Bb
Gm7
Am7
Bb
Bdim
C7
Bb
Am7
Gm7
shine the light Phil - a - del-phi - a - free - dom I love - ove - ove
To Coda
Guitar Tacet
F
you, yes I do

Verse 2. If you choose to, you can live your life alone
Some people choose the city,
Some others choose the good old family home
I like living easy without family ties
'Til the whippoorwill of freedom zapped me
Right between the eyes

Repeat Chorus

ROCKET MAN
(I Think It's Going To Be A Long Long Time)

Moderately slow, with a beat

Words and Music by ELTON JOHN and BERNIE TAUPIN

Eb
Bb/D
Cm
Cm7/Bb
F/A
F/C
on such a time - - less flight.
F
Cm7/F
Bb
And I think it's gon-na be a long long time
Eb
Bb
till touch-down brings me 'round a-gain to find I'm not the man they think I am at home
Eb
Bb/D
C7
Oh no no no, I'm a rock-et man.

Eb
Bb
Eb
To Coda
Rock-et man burn - ing out his fuse up here a - lone.
Eb/Bb
Gm7
Mars ain't the kind of place to
mf
C9
Gm7
C7
raise your kids,
In fact it's cold as hell.
Eb
Bb/D
Cm
Cm/Bb
F/A
F/C
And there's no - one there to raise them if you did.

F
Gm7
C7
C11
C7
And all this sci - ence I don't un - der - stand.
Gm7
C7
C11
Eb
Bb/D
It's just my job five days a week. A rock - et man,
Cm7
Cm7/Bb
F/A
F/C
F
Cm7/F
D.S. al Coda
A rock - et man.
gradual cresc.
CODA
Eb
Bb
Eb
Bb
Repeat and Fade
And I think it's gon - na be a long, long time.

SACRIFICE

Words and Music by ELTON JOHN
and BERNIE TAUPIN

Dm G Am F

In - to the boun - dary ___ of each ___ mar - ried man. ___
We lose ___ di - rec - tion, ___ no stone ___ un - turned. ___

G Am F

Sweet de - ceit comes call - in' ___ and neg - a - tiv - i - ty lands. ___
No tears ___ to damn ___ you ___ when jeal - ous - y burns. ___

G C F(add9)

Cold, ___ cold heart ___ hard done ___ by you. ___

Dm7 G C F(add9)

Some things ___ look - in' bet - ter ba - by just pass - in' through. ___

G
C
F
And it's no sac - ri - fice, just a sim - ple word.
It's two hearts liv -
G
C
- ing in two sep - a - rate worlds.
But it's no
Dm/C
sac - ri - fice, no sac - ri - fice,
it's no sac -
Em
F
F/G
To Coda
C
Em7
ri - fice at all.

1 F(add9) F/G 2 F(add9) C F

Dm7 G C F Dm7 G

D.S. al Coda

Cold, _ cold heart _

CODA

C F Dm G

No sac - ri - fice ___ at all.

C F Dm G

Repeat and Fade

No sac - ri - fice ___ at all.

SOMEONE SAVED MY LIFE TONIGHT

Words and Music by ELTON JOHN
and BERNIE TAUPIN

A
C
A/C♯
an - y - more. We've all gone cra - zy late - ly, my friends out there roll - in' round the
G/D
D7
Chorus
C
G/B
Am7
base - ment floor. And some-one saved my life to - night, sug - ar bear.
C
G/B
Am7
C
G/B
You al - most had your hooks in me did - n't you dear You near - ly had me roped and tied,
C
A7/C♯
G/D
A/E
al - tar bound, hyp - no - tised, sweet free - dom whis - pered in my ear. You're a but - ter - fly, and

C
A7/C#
G/D
B
butter-flies are free to fly, Fly a-way high-a-way bye
C
G/B
Am7
F
G/D
bye.
mf
C
G/D
C
To Coda last time
A7
G/B
Em
And I would have walked head on in-to the deep end of a riv-er, cling-ing to your stocks and bonds, pay-ing your

Verse 2. I never realized the passing hours
Of evening showers,
A slip noose hanging in my darkest dreams.
I'm strangled by your haunted social scene
Just a pawn out-played by a dominating queen.
It's four-o-clock in the morning
Damn it!
Listen to me good.
I'm sleeping with myself tonight
Saved in time, thank God my music's still alive.

To Chorus

SORRY SEEMS TO BE THE HARDEST WORD

Words and Music by ELTON JOHN
and BERNIE TAUPIN

Cm
Bb/F
Cm7(add 9)
F
What do I do to make you want me
What have I got-ta do to be heard
Bb
Am7-5
D7
Gm
Gm7(add 9)
Cm7(add 9)
What do I say when it's all o - ver
F
Bb
F
Eb/G
D/F#
Sor - ry seems to be the hard - est word.
It's sad it's so sad
(it's so sad)
Bb/F
Em7-5
Cm/Eb
D7
Gm
Am7-5
D7
It's a sad sad sit - u - a - tion
And it's get - ting more and more ab - surd

Eb/G
D/F#
Bb/F
C7/E
Eb
It's sad it's so sad
(it's so sad)
Why can't we talk it o-ver
Al-ways seems to me that
Cm7
D7
To Coda
Gm
Cm
sor-ry seems to be the hard-est word
F7
Eb
F7
Bb
Am7-5
D7
Gm
Cm
Cm7
F7
Bb
F/A
D.C. al Coda
CODA
Gm
Bb/F
word. What do I do to make you love

Cm7(add 9)
F7
Bb
me
What have I got to do to be heard.
Gm
Cm
Am7-5
D7-9
What do I do when light - ning strikes me
What have I got to do
Gm
Cm
Am7-5
D7
Bb
Ebm7-5
What have I got to do
Sor - ry seems to be the hard - est word.
Cm/Eb
Gm/D
Am7-5
D7sus
D7
Gm(add 9)

YOUR SONG

Slow, but with a beat

Words and Music by ELTON JOHN and BERNIE TAUPIN

Eb
Fm7
1
Ab
Bb
Bbsus
Bb
I'd buy a big house where we both could live.
My gift is my song and
It's for peo-ple like you, that keep it turned on.
Yours are the sweet-est eyes
2
Ab
Eb
Ab/Eb
Eb
Bb/D
Cm
this one's for you.
I've ev-er seen.
3. 6. And you can tell ev-'ry-bod-y
Fm7
Ab
Bb/D
Cm
This is your song.
It may be quite sim-ple but,
Fm7
Ab
Last time to Coda
Cm
Cm/Bb
now that it's done,
I hope you don't mind, I hope you don't mind

Cm/A
Ab6
Eb/G
Ab6
that I put down in words.
How won - der - ful life is while
rit.
Ab
Bb
Bbsus
Bb
D.S. al Coda
you're in the world.
a tempo
CODA
Cm
Cm/Bb
Cm/A
Ab6
7.8. I hope you don't mind, I hope you don't mind that I put down in words,
How
Eb/G
Ab6
1
Ab
Bb
Bbsus
Bb
won - der - ful life is while you're in the world.
rit.
a tempo
2
Ab
Eb
Ab/Eb
Bb/Eb
Ab/Eb
Eb
you're in the world.
a tempo